THE BIG BOOK OF EARLY ROCK 'N' ROLL

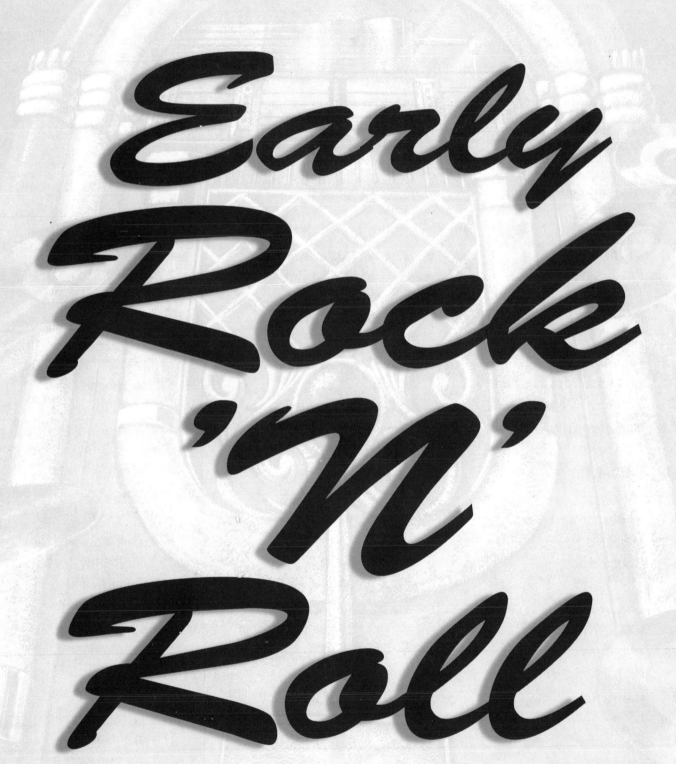

Early Rock 'N' Roll

ISBN 0-7935-9495-2

HAL·LEONARD®
CORPORATION

7777 W. BLUEMOUND RD. P.O. BOX 13819 MILWAUKEE, WI 53213

Visit Hal Leonard Online at
www.halleonard.com

Early Rock 'N' Roll

ALONG CAME JONES

Words and Music by JERRY LEIBER
and MIKE STOLLER

1. I
2. (Com–)
3. (I)

plopped down in my ea-sy chair___ and turned on chan-nel
mer-cial came on so I got up___ to get my-self a
got so bugged I turned it off___ and turned on a-noth-er

two.
snack.
show,

A bad gun sling-er called Sal-ty Sam was a-
You should have seen what was go-in' on by the
but there was the same old shoot-'em-up and the

Repeat bars for 3rd verse only

tied her up. And then? He turned on the buzz–saw. And
tied her up. And then? He lit the fuse to the dynamite. And
tied her up. And then? He threw her on the railroad track. And
then? A train started coming. And

then? And then? And then a-

a tempo
tacet

A♭ 4fr.

long came— Jones,—

E♭7

tall thin— Jones;—

APACHE

By JERRY LORDAN

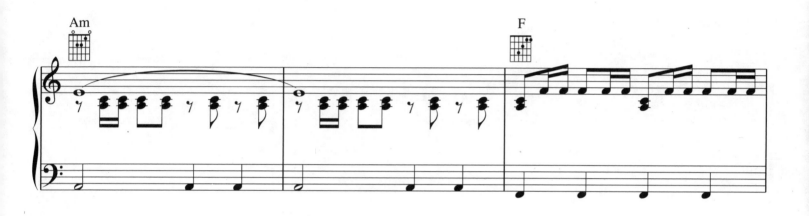

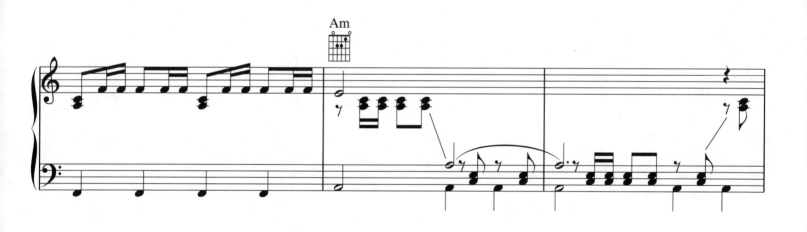

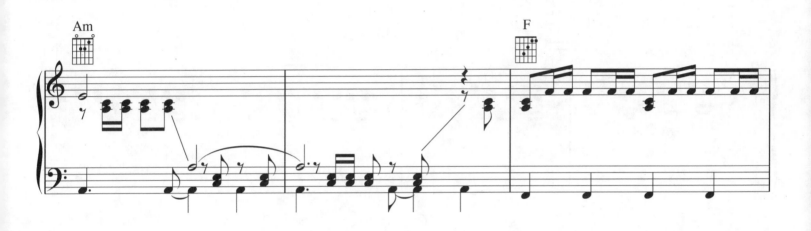

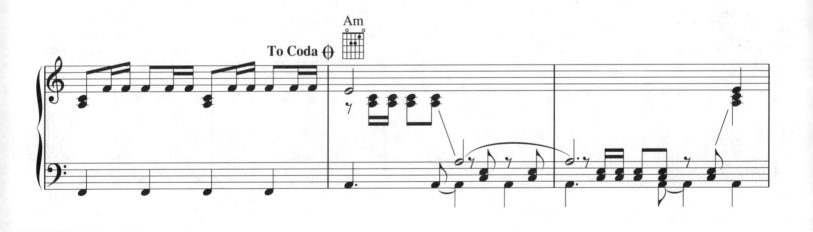

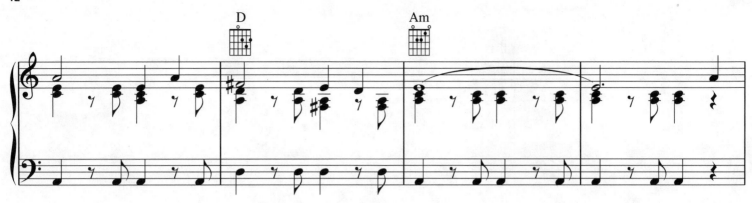

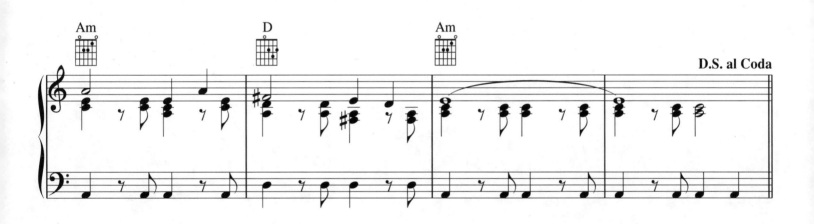

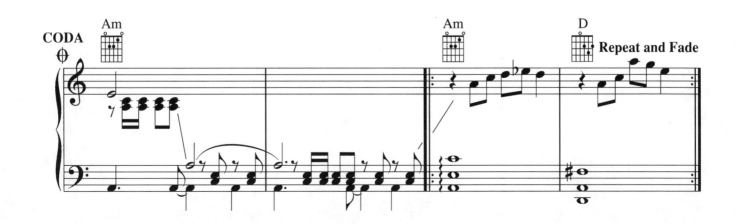

AT THE HOP

Words and Music by ARTHUR SINGER,
JOHN MADARA and DAVID WHITE

Ba ba ba ba, Ba ba ba ba, Ba ba ba ba, Ba ba ba ba, at the hop. Well, you can

ARE YOU LONESOME TONIGHT?

Words and Music by ROY TURK
and LOU HANDMAN

AT MY FRONT DOOR

Words and Music by JOHN C. MOORE
and EWART G. ABNER, JR.

BLUEBERRY HILL

Words and Music by AL LEWIS,
LARRY STOCK and VINCENT ROSE

BLACK DENIM TROUSERS AND MOTORCYCLE BOOTS

Words and Music by JERRY LEIBER
and MIKE STOLLER

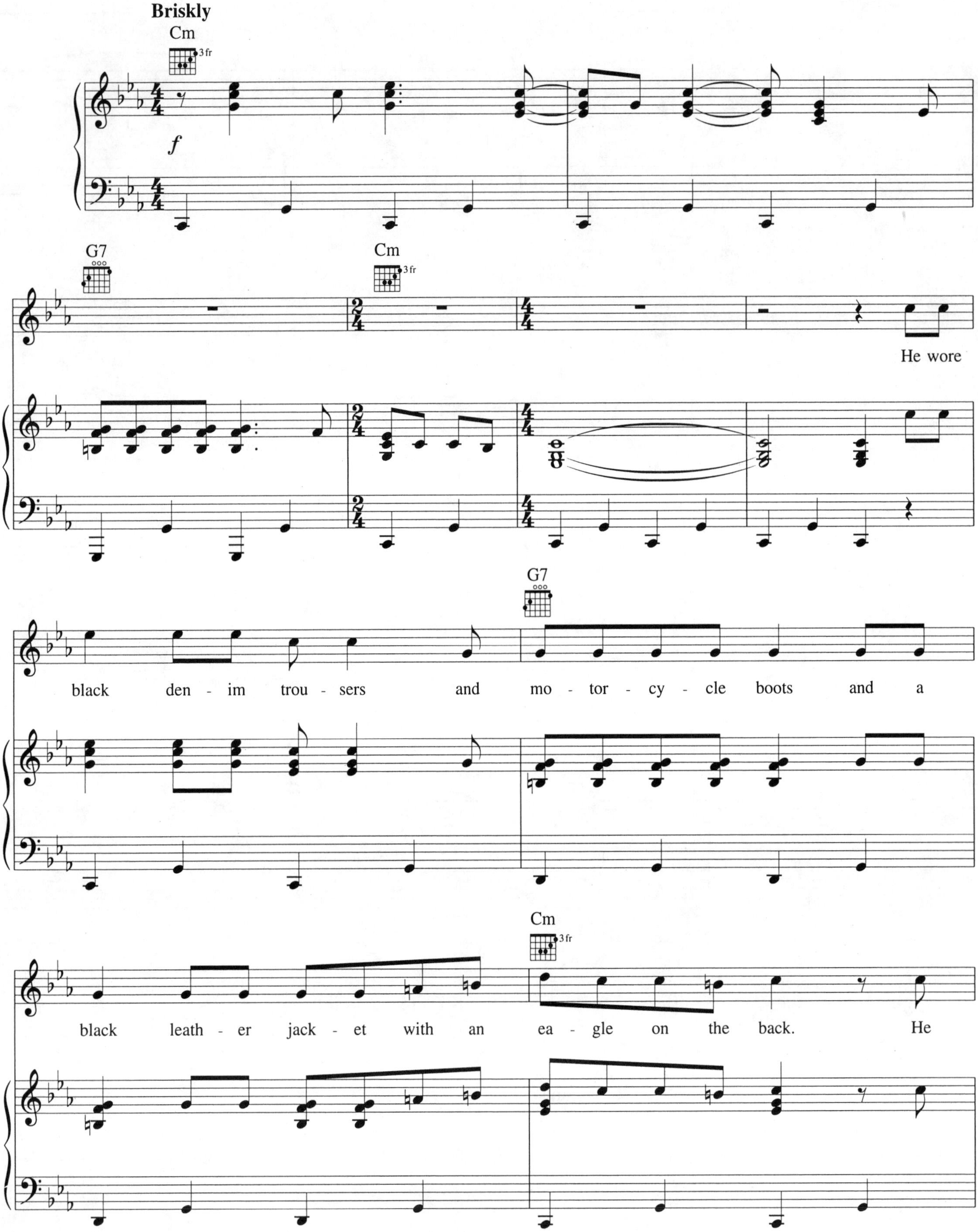

Briskly
Cm
3 fr
f
G7
Cm
3 fr
He wore
G7
black den - im trou - sers and mo - tor - cy - cle boots and a
Cm
3 fr
black leath - er jack - et with an ea - gle on the back. He

had a hopped - up cy - cle that took off like a gun. That
could - n't find the cy - cle that took off like a gun, and they

fool was the ter - ror of high-way one - o - one.

BO DIDDLEY

Words and Music by
ELLAS McDANIEL

Brightly *(a la Calypso)*

Bo Did-dley'll buy ba-by a dia-mond ring,

If that dia-mond ring don't shine, ___

He's gon-na take it to a pri-vate eye.

To make his pret-ty ba-by a Sun-day hat.____

Won't you come to my house and rack that bone,____

Take my ba-by all the way from home. Look at that bo-do, Oh,

where's he been,___ Up to your house and gone a-gain.

Bo Did-dl-ey, Bo Did-dl-ey, have you heard,___

Repeat and Fade

My ___ pret-ty ba-by said she was a bird.

BOBBY SOX TO STOCKINGS

Words and Music by RUSSELL FAITH,
CLARENCE WAY KEHNER and RICHARD DiCICCO

BOBBY'S GIRL

Words and Music by GARY KLEIN
and HENRY HOFFMAN

BONY MORONIE

Words and Music by
LARRY WILLIAMS

CAN'T HELP FALLING IN LOVE

Words and Music by GEORGE DAVID WEISS,
HUGO PERETTI and LUIGI CREATORE

CALENDAR GIRL

Words and Music by HOWARD GREENFIELD
and NEIL SEDAKA

49

CHANTILLY LACE

Words and Music by
J.P. RICHARDSON

54

DREAM BABY
(How Long Must I Dream)

Words and Music by
CINDY WALKER

I'm dream-in' of you   That won't do

Dream ba-by,   make __ me stop my dream-in'   You can make my dreams_ come

true   Sweet   dream

ba - by   Sweet

CHARLIE BROWN

Words and Music by JERRY LEIBER
and MIKE STOLLER

walks in the class - room cool and

slow? Who calls the Eng - lish

teach - er dad - dy - o? Char - lie

"Why is ev - ry -

bo - dy al - ways pick - in' on me?"

F7

D.S. %al Coda

Coda F

(Tacet when sung

)

DANCING IN THE STREET

Words and Music by MARVIN GAYE,
IVY HUNTER and WILLIAM STEVENSON

Call - ing out ___ a - round ___ the world, ___ are you
in - vi - ta - tion a - cross the na - tion, a

read - y for a brand new beat? ___ Sum - mer's here ___ and the
chance for folks to meet. ___ There'll be laugh - ing, sing - ing ___ and

time is right ___ for danc - ing in the street. ___ They're danc - ing in Chi -
mu - sic swing - ing, danc - ing in the street. ___ Phil - a - del - phia, P. A.,

EV'RYBODY'S SOMEBODY'S FOOL
(Everybody's Somebody's Fool)

Words and Music by JACK KELLER
and HOWARD GREENFIELD

EVERYDAY

Words and Music by NORMAN PETTY
and CHARLES HARDIN

Ev - 'ry day it's a - get - tin' clos - er,
Ev - 'ry day it's a - get - tin' fast - er,

go - ing fast - er than a roll - er coast - er.
ev - 'ry - one said "Go on up and ask her." Love like

yours will tru - ly come my way.

FRIENDLY PERSUASION

Words by PAUL FRANCIS WEBSTER
Music by DIMITRI TIOMKIN

FOOLISH LITTLE GIRL

Words and Music by HOWARD GREENFIELD
and HELEN MILLER

Spoken: You broke his heart and made him cry, and he's been blue since then. Now he's found somebody new, and you want him back again.

Moderate Rock

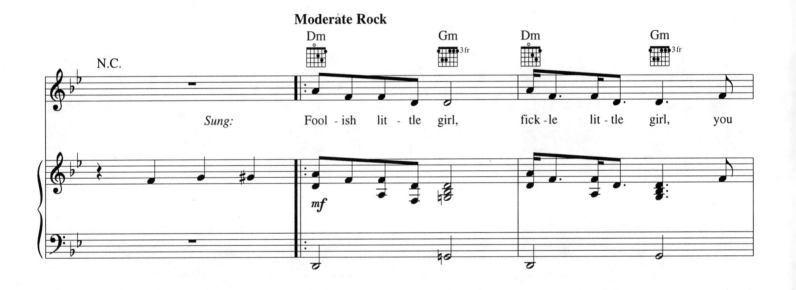

Sung: Fool- ish lit - tle girl, fick -le lit - tle girl, you

did-n't want him when he want- ed you. _____ He's found an-oth- er love; it's

You fool-ish lit-tle girl, fick-le lit-tle girl, you did-n't want him when he want-ed you. _____ He's

GEORGIA ON MY MIND

Words by STUART GORRELL
Music by HOAGY CARMICHAEL

Mel - o - dies bring mem - o - ries that lin - ger in my

heart. _____ Make me think of Geor - gia, why

did we ev - er part? _____ Some sweet day when

GOOD LUCK CHARM

Words and Music by AARON SCHROEDER
and WALLY GOLD

FOR YOUR PRECIOUS LOVE

Words and Music by ARTHUR BROOKS,
RICHARD BROOKS and JERRY BUTLER

Slowly, with expression

Your pre - cious love_____ means more to me_____

Than an - y love could ev - er be._____ For when I want - ed you,_____ I

was so lone - ly___ and so___ blue, For that's___ what love will do.___ And dar - ling,

GOODNIGHT, SWEETHEART, GOODNIGHT

Words and Music by JAMES HUDSON
and CALVIN CARTER

GRADUATION DAY

Words by NOEL SHERMAN
Music by JOE SHERMAN

94

GREAT BALLS OF FIRE

Words and Music by OTIS BLACKWELL
and JACK HAMMER

THE GREAT PRETENDER

Words and Music by
BUCK RAM

GUITAR BOOGIE SHUFFLE

By ARTHUR SMITH

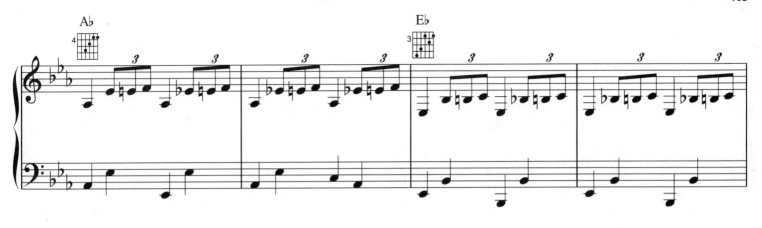

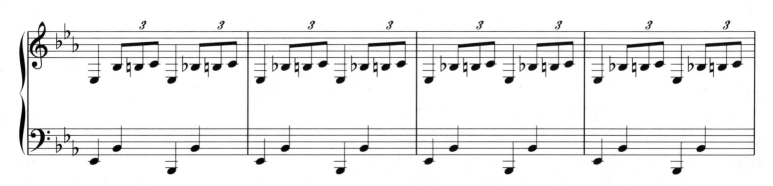

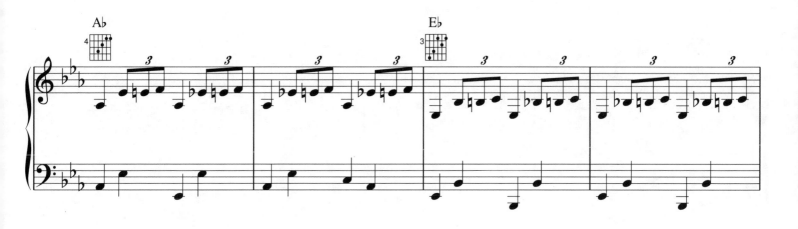

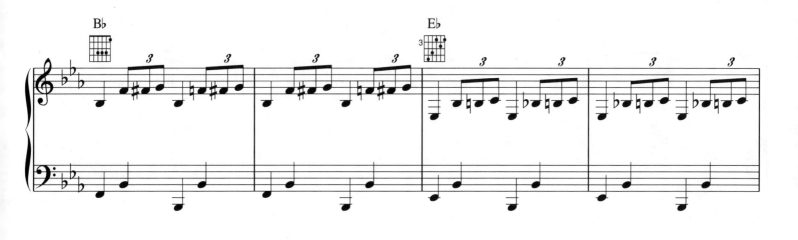

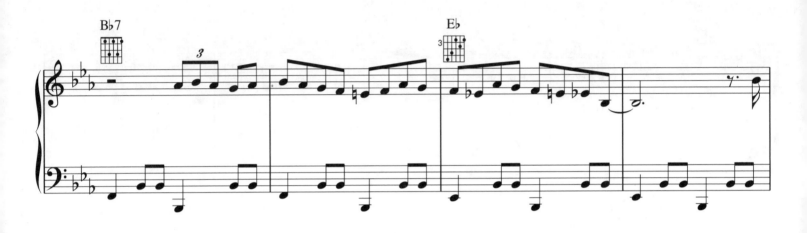

THE GREEN DOOR

Words and Music by BOB DAVIE
and MARVIN MOORE

HAPPY, HAPPY BIRTHDAY BABY

Words and Music by MARGO SYLVIA
and GILBERT LOPEZ

HEATWAVE
(Love Is Like a Heatwave)

Words and Music by EDWARD HOLLAND,
LAMONT DOZIER and BRIAN HOLLAND

Lyrics beneath the staves:

When-ev-er I'm | with him | some-thing in-
calls my name, | stare in-to space, | soft,_ tears_ all
| yeah, | yeah, | yeah,_ whoa

side _____ | starts_ to burn-in'___
low, sweet and plain,__ | I feel, yeah
o-ver my face; | I can't ex-plain it,__ don't un-der-
ho. | Yeah, yeah, | yeah,

HE'S A REBEL

Words and Music by
GENE PITNEY

try the things they've nev-er done, And just be-cause of that they

say:_____ He's a reb-el, and he'll

nev-er ev-er be an-y good, He's a reb-el, 'cause he

nev-er ev-er does what he should, Well, just be-cause he does-n't do what

HEARTS OF STONE

Words and Music by EDDY RAY
and RUDY JACKSON

Hearts made of stone _____ will nev - er break, _____

For the love you have for them, _____ they just won't take.

You can ask them, please, _____ please, please, please break _____

__ And all of your love _____ is there to take.

Yes, hearts of stone _____ will cause you pain, _____

Al - though you love them, _____ they'll stop you just the same.

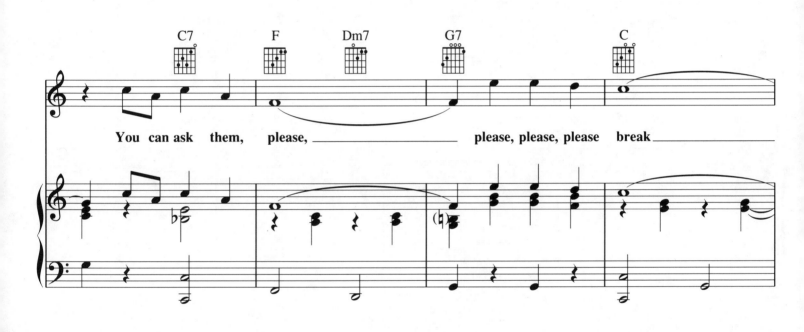

You can ask them, please, _____ please, please, please break _____

__ And all of your love _____ is there to take.

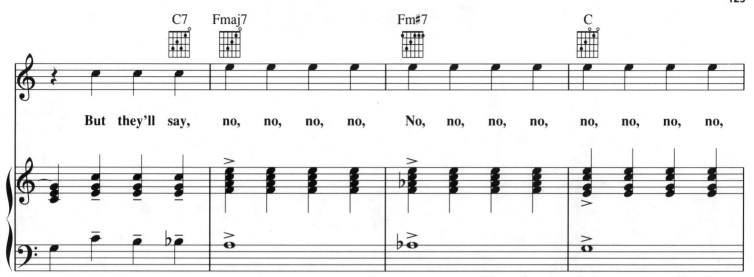

But they'll say, no, no, no, no, No, no, no, no, no, no, no, no,

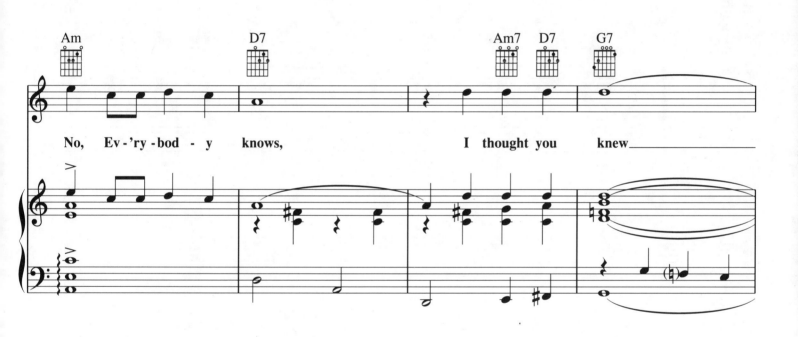

No, Ev-'ry-bod-y knows, I thought you knew_____

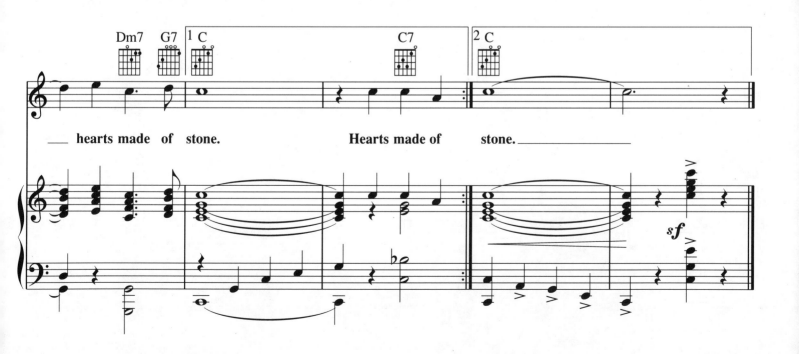

___ hearts made of stone. Hearts made of stone._____

HELLO MARY LOU

Words and Music by GENE PITNEY
and C. MANGIARACINA

Moderately

I ALMOST LOST MY MIND

Words and Music by
IVORY JOE HUNTER

I WANT YOU, I NEED YOU, I LOVE YOU

Words by MAURICE MYSELS
Music by IRA KOSLOFF

Hold me close, hold me tight; make me thrill with de-light. Let me know where I stand from the

start. I Want You, I Need You, I Love You with all my

heart. Ev-'ry time that you're near all my cares dis-ap-pear. Dar-ling,

I'LL BE HOME

Words and Music by FERDINAND WASHINGTON
and STAN LEWIS

JAILHOUSE ROCK

Words and Music by JERRY LEIBER
and MIKE STOLLER

1. The war - den threw a par - ty in the
2.-5. *(See additional lyrics)*

coun - ty jail. ___ The pris - on band was there and they be -

gan to wail. The band was jump - in' and the joint be -

To Coda

Additional Lyrics

2. Spider Murphy played the tenor saxophone
   Little Joe was blowin' on the slide trombone.
   The drummer boy from Illinois went crash, boon, bang;
   The whole rhythm section was the Purple Gang.
   (Chorus)

3. Number Forty-seven said to number Three:
   "You're the cutest jailbird I ever did see.
   I sure would be delighted with your company,
   Come on and do the Jailhouse Rock with me."
   (Chorus)

4. The sad sack was a-sittin' on a block of stone,
   Way over in the corner weeping all alone.
   The warden said: "Hey, Buddy, don't you be no square,
   If you can't find a partner, use a wooden chair!"
   (Chorus)

5. Shifty Henry said to Bugs: "For heaven's sake,
   No one's lookin', now's our chance to make a break."
   Bugsy turned to Shifty and he said: "Nix, nix;
   I wanna stick around a while and get my kicks."
   (Chorus)

IT'S JUST A MATTER OF TIME

Words and Music by CLYDE OTIS,
BROOK BENTON and BELFORD HENDRICKS

IT'S NOW OR NEVER

Words and Music by AARON SCHROEDER
and WALLY GOLD

IT'S SO EASY

Words and Music by BUDDY HOLLY
and NORMAN PETTY

KANSAS CITY

Words and Music by JERRY LEIBER
and MIKE STOLLER

LITTLE DARLIN'

Words and Music by
MAURICE WILLIAMS

(May be spoken over repeat:)

My dear, I need your love to call my own
And never do wrong; and to hold in mine your little hand.
I'll know too soon that I'll love again.
Please come back to me.

THE LITTLE OLD LADY
(From Pasadena)

Words and Music by DON ALTFELD
and ROGER CHRISTIAN

Moderately, with a beat

The lit-tle old la-dy from Pas-a-de-na
see her on the strip don't try to choose her.
see her all the time, just get-tin' her kicks now,

(Go Gran-ny, go, Gran-ny, go, Gran-ny, go. __)
has a pret-ty lit-tle flow-er bed of
You might have a go-er, but you'll
with her four speed stick and a

LITTLE SISTER

Words and Music by DOC POMUS
and MORT SHUMAN

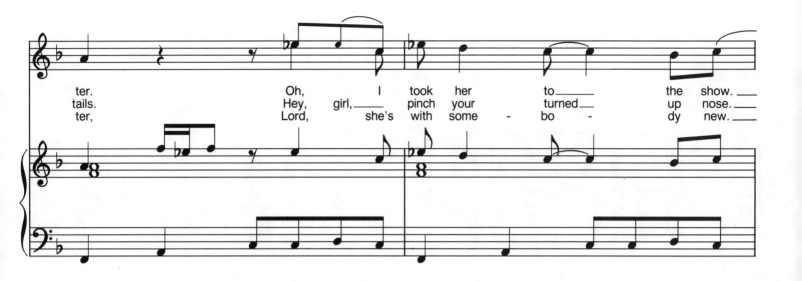

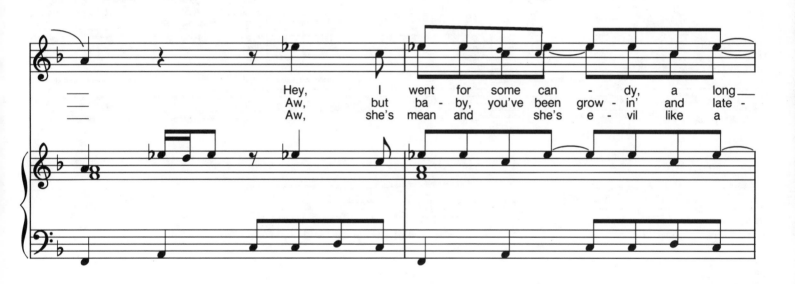

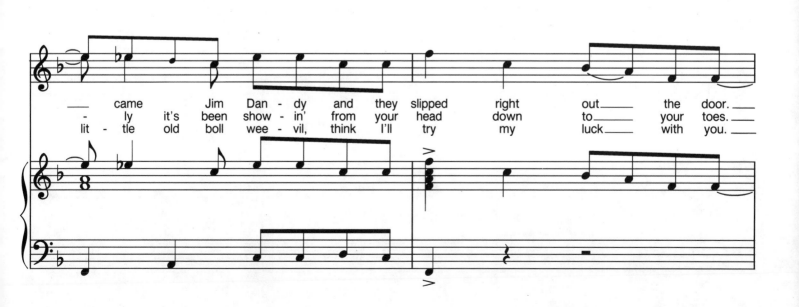

LONELY TEARDROPS

Words and Music by BERRY GORDY,
GWEN GORDY FUQUA and TYRAN CARLO

LOVE ME

Words and Music by JERRY LEIBER
and MIKE STOLLER

LOVE POTION NUMBER 9

Words and Music by JERRY LEIBER
and MIKE STOLLER

MAYBE BABY

By NORMAN PETTY
and CHARLES HARDIN

Moderate Country beat

May-be, ba-by, I'll have you.____ May-be ba-by, you'll be true.____

May-be, ba-by, I'll have you____ for me.____

It's fun-ny, hon-ey; you don't care.____ You nev-er lis-ten to my prayer.____
Instrumental

171

LOVING YOU

Words and Music by JERRY LEIBER
and MIKE STOLLER

*Even eighth notes.

MONEY
(That's What I Want)

Words and Music by BERRY GORDY
and JANIE BRADFORD

Moderate rock

1. The best___ things in life are free,___
2. Your lov - in' give me a thrill,___
3.4. Mon - ey don't get ev - 'ry thing it's true,___

MR. LEE

Words and Music by HEATHER DIXON, HELEN GATHERS,
JANICE POUGHT, LAURA WEBB and EMMA RUTH POUGHT

MY GUY

Words and Music by
WILLIAM "SMOKEY" ROBINSON

RAINDROPS

Words and Music by
DEE CLARK

NO PARTICULAR PLACE TO GO

Words and Music by
CHUCK BERRY

ON BROADWAY

Words and Music by BARRY MANN, CYNTHIA WEIL,
MIKE STOLLER and JERRY LEIBER

ONE FINE DAY

Words and Music by GERRY GOFFIN
and CAROLE KING

One _____ fine   day _____
The   arms   I   long   for ____
One _____ fine   day _____

you'll   look   at   me, _____
will   o - pen   wide, _____
we'll   meet   once   more, _____

and   you will   know ___ our   love   was   meant _____ to
and   you'll be   proud ___ to   have   me   walk - ing by
and   then you'll want ___ the   love   you   threw   a - way

READY TEDDY

Words and Music by JOHN MARASCALCO
and ROBERT BLACKWELL

Bright tempo

Read-y, set, go, man, go, I got a gal that I love so. I'm

read - y read - y read - y Ted - dy. I'm

read - y read - y read - y Ted - dy. I'm

POISON IVY

Words and Music by JERRY LEIBER
and MIKE STOLLER

RETURN TO SENDER

Words and Music by OTIS BLACKWELL
and WINFIELD SCOTT

SEE YOU LATER, ALLIGATOR

Words and Music by
ROBERT GUIDRY

C6

with an - oth - er man to - day. ___
near - ly made me lose my head. ___
You know my love is just for you. ___
I know you meant it just for play. ___

G7

When I asked her what's the mat - ter;
But the next time that I saw her,
Won't you say that you'll for - give me,
Don't you know you real - ly hurt me,

C6

This is what I heard her say. }
Re - mind - ed her of what she said. }
And say your love for me is true. }
And this is what I have to say. }

no chord

See you lat - er, al - li -

C6

ga - tor,

3

af - ter 'while ___ croc - o - dile; ___

RIP IT UP

Words and Music by ROBERT A. BLACKWELL
and JOHN S. MARASCALCO

SH-BOOM
(Life Could Be a Dream)

Words and Music by JAMES KEYES, CLAUDE FEASTER,
CARL FEASTER, FLOYD McRAE and JAMES EDWARDS

SHOP AROUND

Words and Music by BERRY GORDY
and WILLIAM "SMOKEY" ROBINSON

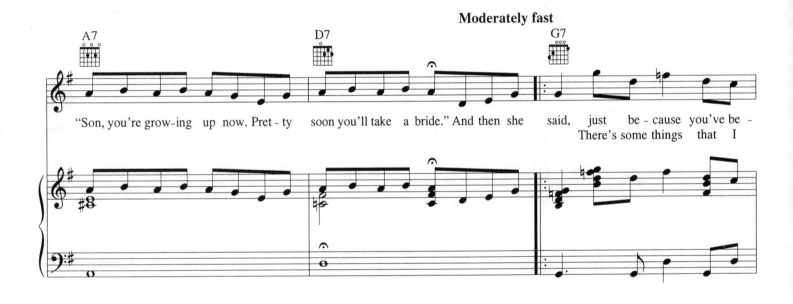

D.S. al Coda

CODA

Make sure that her love is true __ now. I hate to see you feel - in'

sad __ and blue now. __ My ma - ma told me you bet - ter shop a -

N.C.

Repeat and Fade

round. __

STAND BY ME

Words and Music by BEN E. KING,
JERRY LEIBER and MIKE STOLLER

SILHOUETTES

Words and Music by FRANK C. SLAY JR.
and BOB CREWE

SIXTEEN CANDLES

Words and Music by LUTHER DIXON
and ALLYSON R. KHENT

SIXTEEN TONS

Words and Music by
MERLE TRAVIS

Chorus

SLEEPWALK

By SANTO FARINA,
JOHN FARINA and ANN FARINA

SLIPPIN' AND SLIDIN'

Words and Music by RICHARD PENNIMAN, EDWIN BOCAGE,
ALBERT COLLINS and JAMES SMITH

Moderately (♪♪ played as ♪³♪)

Slip-pin' and a-slid-in', peep-in' and a-hid-in', been told a long time a-
Oh, __ big con-niv-er, noth-in' but a jiv-er, done got __ hip to your
Oh, __ Ma-lin-da, she's a sol-id send-er, you know you bet-ter sur-
Slip-pin' and a-slid-in', peep-in' and a-hid-in', been told a long time a-

SMOKE GETS IN YOUR EYES
from ROBERTA

Words by OTTO HARBACH
Music by JEROME KERN

STAY

Words and Music by
MAURICE WILLIAMS

Moderately

Dance_____ just a lit-tle bit long-er._____

Please, please, please, please tell__ me that you're go-in' to._____ Now your

dad-dy don't mind,_____ and your mom-my don't mind._____

THE STROLL

Words and Music by CLYDE OTIS
and NANCY LEE

With a moderately strong rock beat

Come, let's stroll, _____ stroll a - cross the floor ___

Come, let's stroll, _____ stroll a - cross the floor ___

Now turn a - round, ba - by,

STUPID CUPID

Words and Music by HOWARD GREENFIELD
and NEIL SEDAKA

SURF CITY

Words and Music by BRIAN WILSON
and JAN BERRY

SURFIN' U.S.A.

Music by CHUCK BERRY
Lyric by BRIAN WILSON

TAKE GOOD CARE OF MY BABY

Words and Music by GERRY GOFFIN
and CAROLE KING

(Let Me Be Your)
TEDDY BEAR
from LOVING YOU

Words and Music by KAL MANN
and BERNIE LOWE

Medium Bright Rock

Chorus

1. Ba - by, let me be your lov - in' Ted - dy
2. Ba - by, let me be a - round you ev - 'ry

Bear.
night.

Put a chain a - round my neck ___ and
Run your fin - gers through my hair ___ and and

264

A TEENAGER IN LOVE

Words and Music by DOC POMUS
and MORT SHUMAN

THERE GOES MY BABY

Words and Music by JERRY LEIBER, BENJAMIN NELSON,
LOVER PATTERSON, MIKE STOLLER and GEORGE TREADWELL

There goes my ba - by ___ mov - in' on ___ down the line, ___ won-der-in' where, _ won-der-in' where, _ won-der-in' where she is bound. ___ I broke her heart ___

TELL IT LIKE IT IS

Words and Music by GEORGE DAVIS
and LEE DIAMOND

TILL THEN

Words and Music by GUY WOOD,
EDDIE SEILER and SOL MARCUS

TOO MUCH

Words and Music by LEE ROSENBERG
and BERNIE WEINMAN

TURN ME LOOSE

Words and Music by DOC POMUS
and MORT SHUMAN

Turn me loose, turn me loose, I say, __ This is the first time I ev - er

felt this way. Gon - na get a thou - sand kicks, gon - na kiss a thou - sand chicks, So turn me

loose.   Turn me loose,   turn me

UNDER THE BOARDWALK

Words and Music by ARTIE RESNICK
and KENNY YOUNG

TUTTI FRUTTI

Words and Music by LITTLE RICHARD PENNIMAN
and DOROTHY LA BOSTRIE

26 MILES
(Santa Catalina)

Words and Music by GLEN LARSON
and BRUCE BELLAND

Moderate Rock tempo

Twen - ty six miles a - cross the sea ___

San - ta Ca - ta - li - na is a - wait - in' for me, ___ San - ta Ca - ta - li - na, the

is - land of ___ ro - mance, ___ ro - mance, ___ ro - mance, ___ ro - mance. ___ Wa - ter all a - round it

TWILIGHT TIME

Lyric by BUCK RAM
Music by MORTY NEVINS and AL NEVINS

TWIST AND SHOUT

Words and Music by BERT RUSSELL
and PHIL MEDLEY

UP ON THE ROOF

Words and Music by GERRY GOFFIN
and CAROLE KING

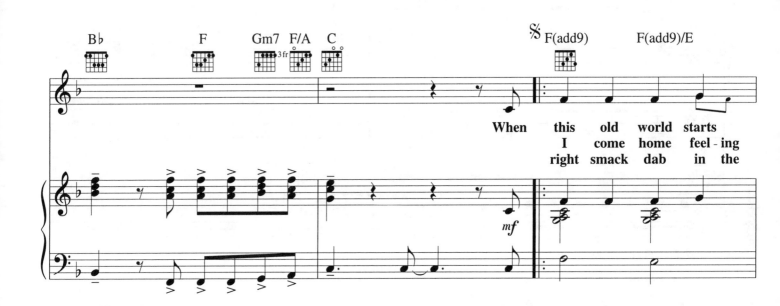

When this old world starts
I come home feel-ing
right smack dab in the

get-tin' me down and peo-ple are just too much for me to
tired__ and down beat I'll go up just where the air is fresh and
mid-dle of town I found a par-a - dise that's trou-ble

304

night the stars put on a show for free

'WAY DOWN YONDER IN NEW ORLEANS

Words and Music by HENRY CREAMER
and J. TURNER LAYTON

THE WATUSI

Words and Music by SHIRLEY HALL,
LESLIE TEMPLE and JAMES JOHNSON

WHERE THE BOYS ARE

Words and Music by HOWARD GREENFIELD
and NEIL SEDAKA

WHY

Words and Music by BOB MARCUCCI
and PETER DeANGELIS

MCA Music Publishing

WHO PUT THE BOMP
(In the Bomp Ba Bomp Ba Bomp)

Words and Music by BARRY MANN
and GERRY GOFFIN

Slowly

I'd like to thank the guy _____ who wrote the

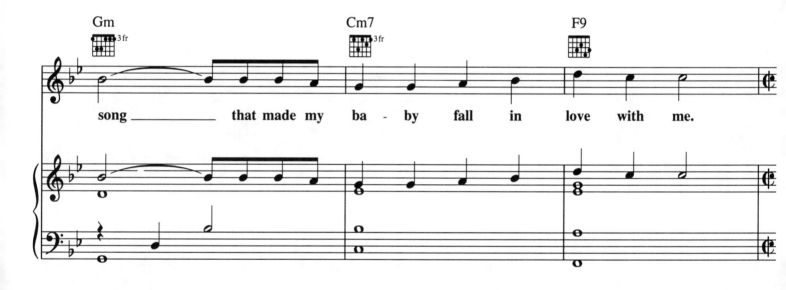

song _____ that made my ba - by fall in love with me.

With a beat

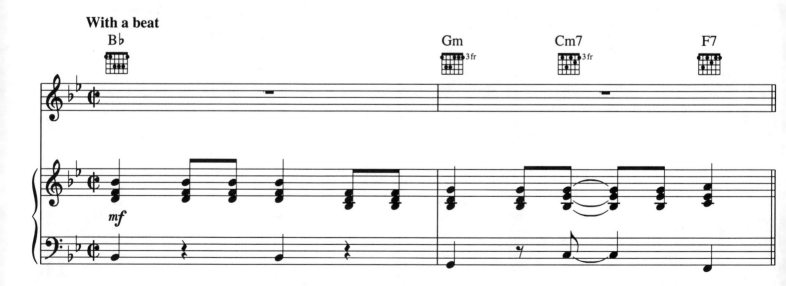

WILL YOU LOVE ME TOMORROW
(Will You Still Love Me Tomorrow)

Words and Music by GERRY GOFFIN
and CAROLE KING

YOU'VE REALLY GOT A HOLD ON ME

Words and Music by
WILLIAM "SMOKEY" ROBINSON

I don't_____ like you,_____ but I_____ love you;
I don't_____ want you,_____ but I_____ need you;
I wan - na leave you,_____ don't wan - na stay you here;

Seems that I'm al - ways_____ think - ing of you._____
Don't wan - na kiss you,_____ but I_____ need to._____
Don't wan - na spend_____ an - oth - er day here._____

YOUNG BLOOD

Words and Music by JERRY LEIBER,
MIKE STOLLER and DOC POMUS

BIG BOOKS OF MUSIC

Our "Big Books" feature big selections of popular titles under one cover, perfect for performing musicians, holiday sing-alongs, and music aficionados. All books are arranged for piano, voice, and guitar, and feature stay-open binding, so the books lie flat without breaking the spine.

THE BIG BOOK OF BROADWAY

Songs from over 50 shows, including *Annie Get Your Gun, Carousel, Company, Guys And Dolls, Les Miserables, South Pacific, Sunset Boulevard,* and more. 76 classics, including: All I Ask Of You • Bali Ha'i • Bring Him Home • Camelot • Don't Cry For Me Argentina • Hello, Young Lovers • I Dreamed A Dream • The Impossible Dream • Mame • Memory • Oklahoma • One • People • Tomorrow • Unusual Way • and more.
00311658............$19.95

BIG BOOK OF CHILDREN'S SONGS

61 songs that children know and love! The P/V/G edition features a categorical listing of songs and ideas for musical and educational activities. Includes: The Alphabet Song • Happy Birthday To You • I Whistle A Happy Tune • It's A Small World • London Bridge • Mickey Mouse March • Old MacDonald Had A Farm • Peter Cottontail • The Rainbow Connection • Supercalifragilisticexpialidocious • This Land Is Your Land • and more!
00359261............$12.95

GREAT BIG BOOK OF CHILDREN'S SONGS

74 classics for kids, including: ABC-DEF-GHI • Beauty And The Beast • Bein' Green • The Brady Bunch • "C" Is For Cookie • The Candy Man • Casper The Friendly Ghost • Everything Is Beautiful • I'm Popeye The Sailor Man • Kum Ba Yah • Let's Go Fly A Kite • The Marvelous Toy • Puff The Magic Dragon • Rubber Duckie • A Spoonful Of Sugar • Take Me Out To The Ballgame • Under The Sea • Won't You Be My Neighbor? • and more.
00310002............$14.95

BIG BOOK OF CHRISTMAS SONGS

An outstanding collection of over 125 all-time Christmas classics, including: Angels We Have Heard On High • Auld Lang Syne • The Boar's Head Carol • Coventry Carol • Deck The Hall • The First Noel • The Friendly Beasts • God Rest Ye Merry Gentlemen • I Heard The Bells On Christmas Day • Jesu, Joy Of Man's Desiring • Joy To The World • Masters In This Hall • O Holy Night • The Story Of The Shepherd • 'Twas The Night Before Christmas • What Child Is This? • and many more.
00311520............$19.95

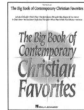

BIG BOOK OF CONTEMPORARY CHRISTIAN FAVORITES

A comprehensive collection of 50 songs, including: Angels • El Shaddai • Friends • The Great Adventure • I Will Be Here • Love In Any Language • Love Will Be Our Home • O Magnify The Lord • People Need The Lord • Say The Name • Turn Up The Radio • Via Dolorosa • Whatever You Ask • Where There Is Faith • and more.
00310021............$19.95

BIG BOOK OF COUNTRY MUSIC

Includes over 60 classic and contemporary country hits: Ain't Going Down ('Til the Sun Comes Up) • Before You Kill Us All • Blue • The Greatest Man I Never Knew • I Can Love You Like That • I've Come to Expect It From You • The Keeper of the Stars • No One Else on Earth • On the Other Hand • One Boy, One Girl • Ring on Her Finger, Time on Her Hands • She's Not the Cheatin' Kind • When You Say Nothing at All • Wild Angels • more.
00310188............$19.95

BIG BOOK OF LATIN AMERICAN SONGS

90 sensational songs from south of the border: The Breeze and I • Cherry Pink and Apple Blossom White • The Coffee Song • Feelings • The Girl from Ipanema • Guantanamera • How Insensitive • La Golondrina • Malagueña • Manha de Carnaval • Piel Canela • Poinciana • Quiet Nights of Quiet Stars • more.
00311562............$19.95

THE BIG BOOK OF JAZZ

75 of the world's greatest jazz classics, including: Autumn Leaves • Bewitched • Birdland • Cherokee • A Fine Romance • Flying Home • Have You Met Miss Jones • Honeysuckle Rose • How High The Moon • (I Can Recall) Spain • I've Got You Under My Skin • Jelly Roll Blues • Lullaby Of Birdland • Morning Dance • A Night In Tunisia • A Nightingale Sang In Berkeley Square • Route 66 • Take The "A" Train • and more.
00311557............$19.95

BIG BOOK OF LOVE AND WEDDING SONGS

Over 80 wedding favorites, including: All I Ask Of You • Anniversary Song • Ave Maria • Could I Have This Dance • Dedicated To The One I Love • Endless Love • Forever And Ever, Amen • Here And Now • Longer • Lost In Your Eyes • So In Love • Something • Sunrise, Sunset • Through The Years • Trumpet Voluntary • The Vows Go Unbroken • You Decorated My Life • and more.
00311567............$19.95

BIG BOOK OF MOVIE AND TV THEMES

Over 90 familiar themes, including: Alfred Hitchcock Theme • Beauty And The Beast • Candle On The Water • Theme From E.T. • Endless Love • Hawaii Five-O • I Love Lucy • Theme From Jaws • Jetsons • Major Dad Theme • The Masterpiece • Mickey Mouse March • The Munsters Theme • Theme From Murder, She Wrote • Mystery • Somewhere Out There • Unchained Melody • Won't You Be My Neighbor • and more!
00311582............$19.95

THE BIG BOOK OF NOSTALGIA

More than 160 of the best songs ever written, complete with a brief history of each song, including: After The Ball • After You've Gone • Anchors Aweigh • Ballin' The Jack • Beale Street Blues • The Bells Of St. Mary's • The Entertainer • Fascination • Give My Regards To Broadway • I Ain't Got Nobody • I Wonder Who's Kissing Her Now • Let Me Call You Sweetheart • Meet Me In St. Louis, Louis • My Wild Irish Rose • Sidewalks Of New York • When Irish Eyes Are Smiling • You Made Me Love You • and more.
00310004............$19.95

THE BIG BOOK OF ROCK

78 of rock's biggest hits, including: Addicted To Love • American Pie • Born To Be Wild • Cold As Ice • Dust In The Wind • Free Bird • Goodbye Yellow Brick Road • Groovin' • Hey Jude • I Love Rock N Roll • Lay Down Sally • Layla • Livin' On A Prayer • Louie Louie • Maggie May • Me And Bobby McGee • Monday, Monday • Owner Of A Lonely Heart • Shout • Walk This Way • We Didn't Start The Fire • You Really Got Me • and more.
00311566............$19.95

THE BIG BOOK OF STANDARDS

86 classics essential to any music library, including: April In Paris • Autumn In New York • Blue Skies • Cheek To Cheek • Heart And Soul • I Left My Heart In San Francisco • In The Mood • Isn't It Romantic? • It's Impossible • L-O-V-E • Lover, Come Back To Me • Mona Lisa • Moon River • The Nearness Of You • Out Of Nowhere • Spanish Eyes • Star Dust • Stella By Starlight • That Old Black Magic • They Say It's Wonderful • The Way We Were • What Now My Love • and more.
00311667............$19.95

BIG BOOK OF SWING

Over 80 swing standards: Air Mail Special • Bye Bye Blackbird • Five Guys Named Moe • Got a Date with an Angel • Honeysuckle Rose • I Hear Music • I've Got My Love to Keep Me Warm • In the Mood • Lazy River • Makin' Whoopee! • Marie • Rag Mop • Satin Doll • A String of Pearls • more.
00310359............$19.95

FOR MORE INFORMATION, SEE YOUR LOCAL MUSIC DEALER, OR WRITE TO:

HAL•LEONARD® CORPORATION

7777 W. BLUEMOUND RD. P.O. BOX 13819 MILWAUKEE, WI 53213

0198